The Handbook: The infancy of SMEs (Small and Medium Enterprises)

This page is requested by Createspace

The Infancy of SMEs: Introduction

Infant stage of SMEs is the earliest stage of a start up business. It is a baby with which you need to cradle it to growing stage for a well-established company.

There are several issues to take care in infant of stage of SMEs. The first issue is registration of the business. SMEs are mostly sole proprietorship and partnership and I propose here SMEs should reach a lawyer to register your company as a limited company. This protects the owner of the business to limited liability without having to pay liabilities at bankruptcy of the business from the personal pocket of the owner.

Next issue is how to cradle your business to growing stage. This issue is to reach breakeven in your business. What is breakeven?

Breakeven is

Revenue + Gross profit x taxation = expenses = Net profit = 0

This handbook to guide your infant business to growing stage and will mainly mention about the two main key jobs of owner in the business to cradle the business to growing stage. What are the two jobs?

One is cost control and the other is pushing sales. Do not start up your business with too many expenses. Cost control is important because if you over spend your capital that is your start-up fund, it is hard to reach breakeven at the earliest time. Next is sales. How can one business start having the first sales? The following will be 9 major industries guiding one by one how to push sales through 4P's (Marketing mix, E. Jereme McCarthy. As mentioned in my previous book, The Handbook, 12 days rescue for the survival of SMEs, 4P's are the guidelines for business to manage. Marketing mix is widely used in large corporations and hereby, I had to mention one thing, SMEs can manage their business through modern management theory which is not limited to large corporations.

To control your cost, you have to have a budget to see thoroughly what you spent in starting up your business. I hereby again urge SMEs starting a business with a small size computerized accounting system with which reports including budgeting can be generated to limit you risk of having too high cost in starting a business.

Hereby I will start with guideline and examples to 9 major industries and the first industry is retail industry.

Retail Industry

Concerning retail industry for SMEs, cost control is one topic. With this, one would need to have a budget to control its cost including the most important item – inventory.

Let's discuss cost control and another key topic pushing sales in SMEs with 4 P's and they are Product, Price, Promotion and Place.

Product

There are two key issues that retail industry SMEs have to be concerned with. One is product and the other is inventory.

For product, SMEs have to search for their selling product and where is or are they be found? The easiest way is through product fairs. Retail SMEs can search for their wanted and desirable products through fairs' booths and sell them in their shop. Price is low when going to buy selling products through fairs as it is in bulks.

(cont.)

Inventory is another topic. Here is the time to mention having your budget in hand to keep in touch with the running of the business and reach breakeven at the shortest time. Inventory has to be calculated to meet the covering of key and most expensive expenses in your shop and they are mainly rental and salary costs. Inventory control has to link with mark up percentage of your product to be sold. If you set your mark up at 50%, you should order and maintain inventory less 50% of revenue and control your inventory to have enough budget to cover your expenses. You have to calculate a budget for a year or more to see how much inventory you have to keep at minimum to breakeven with your spent capital. You as well can use this method to control your ordering of inventory without having ordering too much and get in excessive stock in your business.

Next is price.

(cont.)

Price

This is setting up a mark up for your inventory to sell in your business. Your budget will be a guideline for pricing with which you can check and calculate how much you have to mark up your inventory to cover expenses in your business. An Excel sheet can help with this with all listed expenses and inventory and revenue and can automatically calculate how much mark up do you need to cover up your expenses.

Next is promotion.

Promotion

I hereby suggest SMEs not spending much on promotion. Leaflets can be a cheap way to promote your business and joint promotion could be a nice channel to expand your name recognisation. Discount sales with leaflets distributing on the street can help in pushing sales and one of the method of joint promotion for retail SMEs could be with banks' credit cards promotion booklet with discounts.

Next is Place

Place

This is concerning with the location of your retail shop. Rental cost is a high expense and you need to cover this every month with your projected sales to breakeven in the shortest time frame. I suggest opening in a shopping centre with which rental cost as well covers water and electricity and security. Shopping centre promotes itself and helps with your business.

Hereby I end with retail industry. Next is wholesale industry.

Wholesale Industry

SMEs wholesale industry is different from retail industry. SMEs wholesale companies should focus on product selling, pushing sales at extent. The main reason is wholesale industry has to cover up their high cost in setting up the business and I am going to list out the high cost of wholesale industry and thus can breakeven at its shortest time. I am going to use 4Ps to explain how wholesale SMEs should do to cover up their high cost and breakeven at the shortest time.

Product

Wholesale industry SMEs have to choose what products they need to sell. They buy in bulks and have shipping and delivery costs to bear. If you go to fairs, you might have to order your products with one container. Do not go for one container and order it as bulk goods to reduce delivery and shipping costs. To search for products, one can contact factories or other wholesale industry through the name printed on the product.

There is a channel from Hong Kong Trade Development council and there is lots of product for you to choose. Here I mention again Canton fair is a good place for you to start your business. SMEs wholesale industry has to have varieties in their products to diversify the risk of no sales in certain products. Here comes the topic – inventory. I mentioned this in retail industry and the concept is inventory control through knowing how much you sell in a month. Hereby I mention place.

Place

Do not go for ground shop. To save cost, go to factory buildings with lower cost. There are place for you to move your sales with a second-hand truck. I suggest second-hand truck because is just the reason of cost control.

(cont.)

Promotion

Wholesale industry SMEs can promote through newspaper selling. Leaflets are another kind and is as well using to promote your business. Hire a part-time staff standing on the street at bus stops or terminals of Mass transit railways would help.

Price

Your markup is very important in pricing of your products in wholesale SMEs. You can set levels to giving discount on the higher the quantity one buy the higher discount you give. Make sure your mark up can cover up your sales target to meet your breakeven.

This is wholesale industry SMEs. Next is Service Industry.

Service Industry

I have to introduce two of my handbooks to service industry SMEs. One is The Handbook: Growth of SMEs and the other is the Handbook: The maturity of SMEs. The first one is helping SMEs to grow through diversification and cost control and the other one is risk management. With this, you can plan for your future before setting up your SMEs because service industry is the hardest industry to start up. Now, I am going to introduce through 4Ps for service industry in the infancy period.

Product

The product of service industry SMEs is difficult to sell and you have to prepare yourself that you are not able to have the first business for your company. Besides, offering your basic service, service industry SMEs have to be updated with the society and provide up to date service to your customer. Where can you be informed with up to date services? Magazines, fairs, and association can help.

Place

The office space of service industry SMEs is simple. Find a convenient place with bus stop and or Mass Transit Railway to serve your customer. The price will not be too high and you can easily cover your cost for breakeven at the shortest time.

Promotion

Service industry promotion is the hardest as it is really a milestone to bring in the first business. Offer service package to your clients but you have to calculate accurately what is the mark up for each item in the package. Yellow page, newspaper, magazine of your industry, free newsletter of your own can help. Another will be hiring a marketing firm for telemarketing for your business. This helps in bringing in your business without having "flies" in your office.

Price

Hereby pricing is linked with the above topic promotion with service package offered to clients or tailored made to clients. Collect information from your competitors to see how they charge and in the mean time, you need to protect your pricing by not allowing pricing leakage through your receptionist or sales. Face to face meeting is needed to protect your pricing strategy.

Hereby I end with service industry. Next is F&B industry.

F & B Industry

In my previous books, The Handbook: Growth of SMEs, I have introduced how cost should be calculated to get into profit making environment.

Now is time to talk about how F & B industry SMEs should do in the infancy stage.

Product

The menu of F & B industry SMEs is the key for products. You should set up a large variety menu for your customer to choose but it is difficult as it needs to have enough inventories to cover up the menu for your business. Inventory control has to fit in the total number of dishes that are forecasted to be sold per day. Here comes a computerized accounting system can help. The number of dishes sold per day or in a month can be shown by the system and you can estimate the inventory amount that you need to fit in the menu.

Price

The price of the dishes was mentioned in my published book namely The Handbook: Growth of SMEs. You can offer monthly discount days say for example at 1st and 15th of every month, there is a discount in your restaurant with specialties offering.

Promotion

Now is time for promotion of your SMEs. Tourist map can be a way to promote your business and can not just attract local customers but as well tourists from other countries. It would not be so expensive as possibly this is offered by the tourism department in your government. Check it out if you have one in your country if not ask them to have one.

(cont.)

Place

Rental cost is a key right now in place topic. Presently, there is high cost in rental of shops for your SMEs. Choose a right place at the right spot. Having bus stops and mass transit railway will be a benefit for your SMEs. There will be large amount of customer flow walking across your shop and could attract customers through this. Do not choose right at the spot of the above mentioned places as the rental will be expensive and crowded with people. Choose nearby spots to take the chance of having the flow into your business.

Here is the end of F&B. The next stop is manufacturing industry.

Manufacturing Industry

Here comes manufacturing industry SMEs infancy stage. To start up a factory is not that easy and need to plan for a lot of issues. Machineries, labour, logistic, etc. are the things manufacturing SMEs boss have to think about.

To start with, I am using 4Ps to introduce how manufacturing industry SMEs can do in the infancy stage.

Product

Product in manufacturing industry is not just manufacturing your own product and for sale or trading in foreign countries and in local. It includes manufacturing of orders from customers. This depends on what technology the boss is keen in establishing a factory. If you have the chance with a technology that you are keen in and can do both – one manufacturing your own product and one manufacturing from orders of customers, you have a wide range of business in your SMEs.

(cont.)

Place

There are two major issues in choosing the right place of a manufacturing industry SMEs. One is choosing a site from a factory building and one is building your own factory. The first method is cheaper than the second as the second needs to have a piece of land either from rental or by buying it. Here comes a topic namely logistic. Cargo delivery is important in manufacturing industry and if your site is too far away from delivery from harbors, the cost will be high. One more is airport. If your site is far away from the delivery airport, cargo delivery charge will be high. Calculate your cost in choosing the right place for your business and make sure you are able to choose from the above two methods of technology in manufacturing products.

(cont.)

Promotion

Promotion of manufacturing industry SMEs is not that easy as it is hard to find clients and or sell your products to clients in your market. There is a book namely Enterprise in Hong Kong Trade and Development Council where you can advertise your products to public from foreign and local purchasers. Sell your products in fair at wholesale price with which you can earn profits from your products and at the same time promote your business.

Price

Pricing is hard in manufacturing industry as it involves lots of procedures in the manufacturing process. Make sure you calculate all steps of the manufacturing processes as with labour, raw materials, electricity, machinery, logistic etc. in the pricing. Besides pricing products, manufacturing industry SMEs are exposed to high risk in currency and this involves in risk management of SMEs as mentioned in my previous book: The Handbook: The maturity of SMEs. If you are able to hedge currency risk in your business, you will earn more and able to recover your capital imposed into your business.

Here is manufacturing industry of SMEs. Next stop is construction industry,

Construction Industry

Start up of a construction company as SMEs is not hard and the hardest is how are you going to start with your first project. In my previous book, I have mentioned how to choose projects through present value calculation. Now it is time to start with 4Ps for a construction industry SMEs to start up and cover the costs and breakeven at the earliest time.

Place

Choosing an office space will be nice for a startup. The rental is not that high and you need simple furniture and fixtures and design to make your meeting with customers comfortable and effective.

Product

Product of a construction industry is the service that you offer to clients for constructing a building and or simply build it by yourself. The difference is one offering service and one having the whole project of your own with your own costs. Both ways needs to have labour and hereby will be sub-contractor findings. With this, you less your personal expense and outsource the construction procedures to keep yourself at low risk.

Promotion

Where are you going to promote your new company? Newspaper? No much use. Try yellow pages at low cost. Join with construction association to share experience and get information from members with which you might be able to collaborate with other construction companies to start a project. Real estate agencies are another. They could help in promoting your flats or buildings but make sure they did not over price your pricing if not there might be bubble happened to your site.

(cont.)

Price

Outsourcing your labour cost helps in having a low price and keeps it in high quality materials used in your site. You minus the cost of having high price machineries for construction as from Caterpillar. Management is important here and pricing has to be calculated with PVIF knowing your cash flow as a benchmark and price your space calculated in meter square. Land is the largest cost and you have to estimate the land amortization to cover up your cost with accurate pricing if not in the future, you might lose your profits and not able to cover up the highest cost both for your clients and or yourself if you are providing service or building your own building respectively.

I have not much to mention here with construction industry SMEs and if you wish, try a fair through construction materials to promote your business and find collaborators to move your profits to breakeven in the earliest time.

Next is hotel industry.

Hotel Industry

Hotel industry SMEs is an expensive industry. One who builds a SMEs hotel needs a lot of cash to support the business. In my previous books, I have mentioned either through loans or angel financing to build a hotel. Here comes a problem. How could a SMEs hotel cover up it expenses and capital to breakeven at the shortest time?

I will talk about this with 4Ps step by step to help SMEs hotel to breakeven at the shortest time.

Product

SMEs hotel product is its rooms and restaurants. These two are profit centers and generate cash for the business. For rooms, there must be a briefing in the morning before working to check the room rates of other SMEs hotel to fight for business in the day. The pricing of SMEs hotel could simply comparing room rates with other SMEs hotel and not by calculating with square meters and facilities in the rooms. Next is how can you raise your room rates in comparison with other SMEs hotel? Improve your SMEs hotel into 5 stars hotel as mentioned in my previous book: The handbook: Growth of SMEs and can fight for a higher rate than other SMEs.

The next is restaurants. Menus are important. Most hotels have buffet and a la carte. SMEs hotel restaurant can talk about fast outside delivery to customers. Changes of items in menus are important and it should be from time to time. You can simply add in specialties at certain time for example in summer time, add in Thai food for refreshment of customers with little spicy items in it.

Price

Pricing in SMEs hotel industry consists of several items which include room rate, restaurants, housekeeping and other services like barber shop and gymnasium. Let's talk about them one by one. First is room rate. Competitive Pricing is needed in this section. Your competitors pricing is your standard and you have to rate your room in having competitiveness with your competitive. Restaurants are the next.

(cont.)

I have talk about F&B industry pricing in my previous book: The handbook: Growth of SMEs and it is not that hard with which if your SMEs hotel has a computerized accounting system, it would be easy to calculate the pricing. Next is housekeeping. Laundry in housekeeping in a hotel is often used for long stay customers. Keep the pricing low to attract customers to use your service. Pricing of barber shop and gymnasium could be priced with VIP discount cards and Club member cards respectively. Barber shop in an hotel can gain profits if your stylists can make nice hairstyle and service to customers not just for in house guests but as well as outside customers. Gymnasium is another facility in a hotel. If you have one, use Club Member card through selling them with telemarketing team. Launch a telemarketing team to sell club member card to outside customers and can have discount in restaurants and enjoy services in the hotel.

Place

This is the hardest part of an SMEs hotel setup infancy stage. One has to rent a land or buy a land to build the hotel and if you buy a land, it is possible to help you with angel financing and you have to calculate amortization rate of the land if you buy the land. This will help you to breakeven with your budgeting.

Promotion

Promotion in hotel SMEs has to be handled by Director of Marking and the marketing team with which banquets are handled by them too. To start with your new business, SMEs hotel should collaborate with tourist agencies and then add private promotion to their business. If you have shuttle bus through rental, promotion can be done through having your slogan and image on the shuttle bus. Fair is another way out. If you are able to establish a booth in a tourism fair, it would be profitable for the business to gain knowledge of your SMEs hotel and is a kind of promotion for your business. Mind your promotion cost as you have to cover up the cost of promotion in your product that is through your room rate.

I finish SMEs hotel here and the last stop is academic institution.

Academic Institution

Academic Institutions, I refer to education centers as with my previous books. My previous books mentioned the growth and maturity of education centers and now, I am introducing how an academic Institution can survive and breakeven in their infant stage.

Product

The product of an education centre is their offering programmes. They can be certificates, diplomas, bachelor degree, Master degree and even Doctor or PhD degree. To start with, SMEs education centers have to position themselves with their offered products to candidates. Search for the needs of the market in your region and you can easily position yourself into a startup and able to breakeven SMEs. As mentioned in my previous book, education centre can be online or not online and if you decide to be online education centers, you have to be equipped with technologies and this add to your capital in the SMEs and need more time perhaps to breakeven. Plan for your business first as I am going to mention something in the later part why education centre risk management is important.

Place

Education centers can be in commercial building firstly and then when it breakevens, you can start with your plan to grow in your business. You can move yourself with several financing methods as mentioned in my previous book and develop yourself into a bigger education centre and even an university. Choose a convenient spot with bust stop or mass transit railway for your candidates and your business save time as well.

Price

Pricing in education centre is not complicated. The main cost is the salary of professors, and lecturers. When you set price for your courses, you have to cover the cost of professors and lecturers to make profit. There is always a risk in education centre that there might be enough candidates enrolling in the course offered. Set a contract for professors and lecturers that you need not pay them anything if there are not enough candidates for the course.

(cont.)

This protects you from your risk. If you are an online education centre, the equipments cost has to be covered in your course offered to breakeven. Do not forget there will be depreciation for the equipments and you should calculate detailed how much you have to cover in your courses if you offer courses for the market.

Promotion

Education centre promotion needs to be clear and be detailed enough to let customers to know what course you offered to the market. Just a title is not enough. You should list out specialties on your advertisement if you are using newspapers to promote your products. Go to fair to set up a booth for candidates. Not just having known to people, you are able to find collaborators as well for your business in the infant stage and see if there are any outsourcing courses that you can have from other education centers or universities. Through an education fair, you would be able to reach out universities and have joint programmes with them and upgrade your business with the name of your collaborators' names.

This is the end of this handbook and I wish you all good luck in your business setup in the infancy stage.

www.ingramcontent.com/pod-product-compliance
Lightning Source LLC
Chambersburg PA
CBHW070724180526
45167CB00004B/1606